sew cuddly

JUDY GAUTHIER

12 Plush Minky Projects for Fun & Fashion

TIPS & TECHNIQUES TO CONQUER CUDDLE

C&T PUBLISHING

Text copyright © 2018 by Judy Gauthier

Photography and artwork copyright © 2018 by C&T Publishing, Inc.

PUBLISHER: Amy Marson

CREATIVE DIRECTOR: Gailen Runge

ACQUISITIONS EDITOR: Roxane Cerda

MANAGING EDITOR: Liz Aneloski

EDITORS: Liz Aneloski and Katie Van Amburg

TECHNICAL EDITOR: Helen Frost

COVER/BOOK DESIGNER: April Mostek

PRODUCTION COORDINATOR: Tim Manibusan

PRODUCTION EDITOR: Alice Mace Nakanishi

ILLUSTRATOR: Mary E. Flynn

PHOTO ASSISTANT: Mai Yong Vang

COVER AND STYLE PHOTOGRAPHY by Lucy Glover and
INSTRUCTIONAL PHOTOGRAPHY by Mai Yong Vang
of C&T Publishing, Inc., unless otherwise noted

Published by C&T Publishing, Inc., P.O. Box 1456,
Lafayette, CA 94549

Library of Congress Cataloging-in-Publication Data
Names: Gauthier, Judy, 1962- author.
Title: Sew cuddly : 12 plush Minky projects for fun & fashion -
tips & techniques to conquer Cuddle / Judy Gauthier.
Description: Lafayette, CA : C&T Publishing, Inc., 2018.
Identifiers: LCCN 2017050079 | ISBN 9781617456831 (soft cover)
Subjects: LCSH: Textile crafts. | Plush.
Classification: LCC TT715 .G38 2018 | DDC 745.592/4--dc23
LC record available at https://lccn.loc.gov/2017050079

Printed in China
10 9 8 7 6 5 4 3 2 1

contents

General Tips and Instructions for Minky Cuddle Fabric   5

Using a fabric with stretch • What about shedding? • Appliquéing with minky cuddle
Making sewing with minky cuddle easier • Some essentials for this book

PROJECTS

dedication

I dedicate this book to my mother, who has been deceased for many years. She was my coach, my sewing teacher, and the person that taught me everything about sewing with different substrates. It can be tricky to sew with lots of different types of fabric, and she taught me not to be afraid to try all kinds. As a result, I love to incorporate many textures and fibers into my sewing. That is why I was so excited when plush fabrics came onto the market, along with the sumptuous double gauzes and suede. I knew I had to write a book about this topic. Thanks, Mom, for creating a courageous seamstress.

acknowledgments

I would like to acknowledge all the great people at C&T Publishing for all the work they do with me. I also would like to acknowledge everyone at Shannon Fabrics, especially the sales and market- ing people. They have been extremely helpful in providing supplies and inspiration.

I also need to acknowledge the helpful staff that I have at the shop. They put in extra hours so that I could get this book done. Well done, ladies!

general tips and instructions for minky cuddle fabric

Minky cuddle is the most wonderful fabric to work with: It's soft, forgiving, and very attractive when made into a number of different things. However, like any substrate other than plain cotton, there can be some tricks to working with it. For example, you cannot use an iron with minky cuddle.

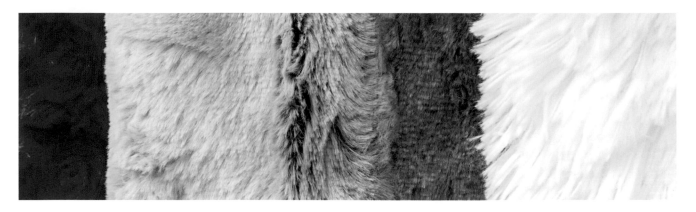

Minky cuddle fabric is made from polyester. It has some stretch and give, but not as much as one might think.

using a fabric with stretch

When sewing with fabric with some give, here are some things to keep in mind.

- Most often, it has more stretch in one direction than the other. Find out where the stretch is, and take this into consideration when cutting, especially when cutting pattern pieces.

- Sometimes, a little stretch can work in your favor. However, make sure not to allow something to be uneven and then decide to stretch it in the end to make up for the unevenness. This won't make for a nice-looking finished product.

- There are ways to keep fabric from stretching, including products that help with this.

How to Keep Fabric from Stretching

- Apply a strip of sticky stabilizer to the seamline. If you don't want the extra bulk after you're done sewing the seam, using a stabilizer that washes away is the perfect solution. A couple that work beautifully are Wash-Away Stitch Stabilizer (by C&T Publishing) and Sulky Sticky Fabri-Solvy Stabilizer.

- Another product that works well is my Tear-Perfect Maker Tape (by C&T Publishing). This tears on a grid, so you can easily tear a ¼˝ strip. Lay the strip right next to the edge that is vulnerable to stretching, and sew a seam there.

  You can easily remove it without leaving any residue, and you can reuse it for the next piece.

- Good old-fashioned stay stitching works every time. Use a longer stitch and sew along the edge of the fabric, usually within the seam allowance so that it doesn't show when the seam is actually made.

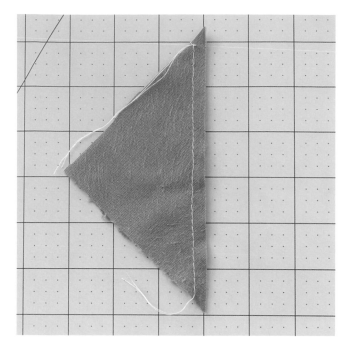

- Apply stabilizer to the entire piece of fabric. This can be tricky, since you cannot use a hot iron on minky cuddle. Stabilizers that stick without having to be heated work well. Adhesive sprays can also be sprayed to the piece of fabric, and then the fabric can be adhered to a stable piece of fabric, such as muslin or nonfusible interfacing. If you use an adhesive spray, make sure you're in a well-ventilated area.

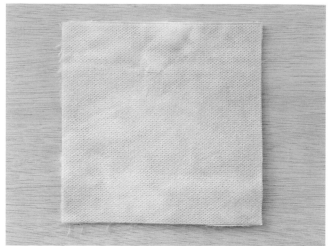

what about shedding?

Many people come into my shop and say that they don't want to work with minky cuddle because it sheds. Well, the shedding is manageable and the end result is so worth any trouble encountered with the fibers.

Shedding does not occur from the fabric itself until it is cut, and stops completely after you shake the fabric and the edges are no longer fresh.

How to Manage Shedding

- If it's a nice day, move the cutting table out into the open air and cut the fabric outdoors. You probably need that vitamin D anyway!

- Handle the fabric gently after cutting, and then move to a door and shake the fabric vigorously outside.

- Apply a wide piece of painter's tape to the fabric where you plan to cut it. Cut across the tape and remove the tape when finished.

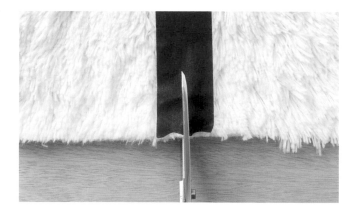

- Use a portable vacuum to suck up the fibers immediately after cutting. You can even vacuum the edge of the piece that you've cut if you have a vacuum that allows you to decrease the amount of suction.

SHAGGY CUDDLE AND FAUX FUR

Shaggy cuddle and faux fur are lovely to work with and have an element of playfulness. Don't shy away from these wonderful products because of the shedding.

- Flip the fabric over to the wrong side. Slip the tip of the scissors under the fabric. Cut the fabric without cutting the fur.

- Part the fabric from the right side with an index card or a comb, and apply wide painter's tape to the nap. It's kind of like parting your hair. Cut along the base fabric.

This works very well. By making a shallow cut, you don't cut the actual fibers, just the fabric that the fibers are attached to. It will still shed a bit, but markedly less.

appliquéing with minky cuddle

If you're a fan of appliqué, doing it with minky cuddle is the most fun—ever.

Since you cannot use an iron, I recommend using a stabilizer where the glue is already activated and does not need to be heat set, such as Wash-Away Stitch Stabilizer (from C&T Publishing) or Sulky Sticky Fabri-Solvy Stabilizer. By using a stabilizer that is already sticky, you can stick it to the appliqué piece and pin or spray it in place. Adhesive sprays work well, but be mindful to use them in a well-ventilated area.

You don't need to finish the edges because minky cuddle doesn't fray! If you are appliquéing something to the cuddle that does fray, use the above directions, and then sew the piece to the cuddle using a zigzag stitch.

making sewing with minky cuddle easier

Sewing with minky cuddle can look intimidating, but if you follow a few simple rules, you won't have any trouble whatsoever.

Always use a walking foot.

As in other fabrics with a nap, the nap tends to go one direction or the other. Have you ever held a piece of velvet or corduroy and noticed that it looked lighter or darker depending on how you held it, or that it looked lighter when you petted it in one direction and darker the opposite direction? That's because fabric with a nap has fibers that stand up. Because of this, they grab each other when two pieces are set right sides together. This grabbing across the fibers causes the fabric to dramatically shift. Using a walking foot helps because there are feed dogs on both sides: under the fabric and over the fabric. This evens out the movement and keeps the fabric from shifting.

Use a longer stitch.

Just like you use a longer stitch when you use a bulkier fabric and multiple layers, do the same with minky cuddle. It makes the fabric run through the machine more smoothly.

Adjust the pressure of the presser foot.

Most machines have this capability. It may help to have a little less pressure on the presser foot, but if this doesn't help, try the opposite! I give you permission to play around.

Remember: Hand basting is not only for your mother.

Yup, she was right when she told you to hand baste. It helps tremendously in keeping the fabrics together. Pins and clips work well too, but you need to pin very frequently and it can cause you to stab yourself, particularly if the pins get lost in the nap. When hand basting, the stitches should be no longer than ⅜˝. *If you're not going to hand baste, then pin very securely.*

(tip) If you're working with a minky cuddle fabric with a longer nap and you need a zipper, put some distance between the zipper and the nap. In the Bundle Me Up Stroller Wrap (page 16), I use a technique for binding the zipper tape before sewing it in. This is not as necessary with the shorter nap fabrics, but for luxe cuddle and faux fur, it's essential.

some essentials for this book

- Each project in this book uses a ⅜˝ seam allowance. However, if you are using a low-nap cuddle, you might be able to use a ¼˝ seam. Use a ¼˝ seam on zippers.

- You will need to download the patterns, print them out, and then make templates from card stock or template plastic from the patterns. All patterns in this book are available to download at:

  tinyurl.com/11312-patterns-download

Important: Transfer all the markings from the pattern pieces and pattern guides to the fabrics before you start sewing.

- Several projects have reversed pieces. Either cut the pieces right sides together or turn over the template for the reversed piece.

- Hand basting is preferred. Pinning is provided as an alternative option, but if you pin instead of basting, make sure to do so very securely.

Zipper Anatomy

Multiple projects in this book have zippers. It is important to keep the following references and wording in mind when working on a project with a zipper.

- A **nonseparating nylon zipper** is the kind used in most of the projects with zippers.

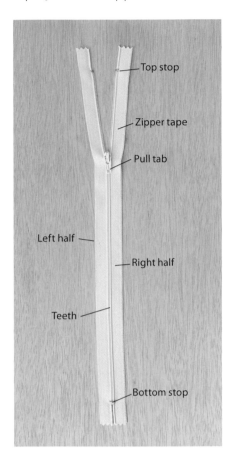

- A **separating zipper** is the kind on a coat or jacket where you put the metal piece at the bottom into the box at the bottom. This zipper is used in the projects Bundle Me Up Stroller Wrap (page 16) and Sleep Sack (page 52).

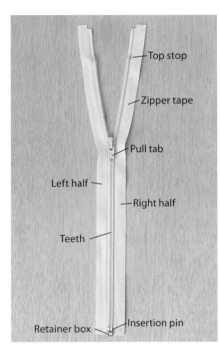

- The **zipper tab** is the part that you pull on when you want to pull the zipper up or down.

- In this book, I talk about the zipper facing you, or the **front side of the zipper**. That is referring to the side of the zipper that has the tab. The opposite side is the back of the zipper.

- When the zipper is facing you, there is a **left half**, a **center**, and a **right half**.

- The **zipper tape** is the part of the zipper made up of fabric alongside the teeth.

Binding with Minky Cuddle

Traditional quilt binding works with minky cuddle. But the wonderful thing about minky cuddle is that you don't have to go through all of the steps for creating the binding that you do with regular cotton fabric. Minky cuddle doesn't ravel. What?? I will say it again: Minky cuddle doesn't ravel. You can use it with raw edges on anything. That said, we can talk about binding.

The Bath Mat (page 48) uses a traditional quilt binding process (see page 10). The *Cuddle Me Cuttlefish* quilt (page 60) uses the raw-edge binding (see Nontraditional Binding, page 11).

TRADITIONAL BINDING

1. Cut strips 2½˝ × width of fabric.

2. With right sides together, place the strips at right angles.

3. Draw a diagonal line across the strips from the upper left corner of the top strip to the lower right corner of the bottom strip. Stitch directly on this line. Trim the corner beyond the stitching.

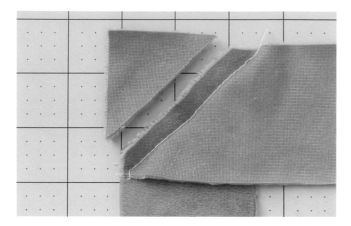

4. Continue to join strips together in this manner until you have enough to bind the entire project. (The number of strips is indicated in the project instructions.)

5. Fold the binding strips in half lengthwise, wrong sides together.

6. Leave a 6˝ tail and pin it securely to the edge of the front, right sides together, keeping the edges even.

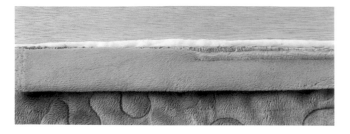

7. Sew to the front, stopping the stitching ¼˝ from the corner. Clip the threads.

8. Pull the binding up, creating a 45° angle.

9. Fold the binding straight down so that it is even with the top edge and the next side. Pivot and continue sewing along the edge.

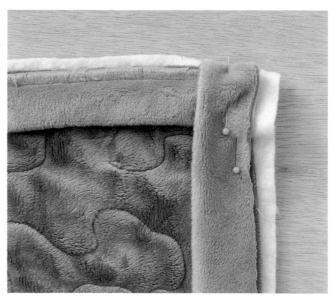

10. Continue around all the sides until you approach the starting point. Stop at least 12˝ from the beginning stitches.

11. Butt the starting end of the binding up against the other end of the binding by folding the pieces back onto themselves and having them meet at the folds. Measure 1″ from the fold on each piece of binding and mark the 1″. Cut at this point.

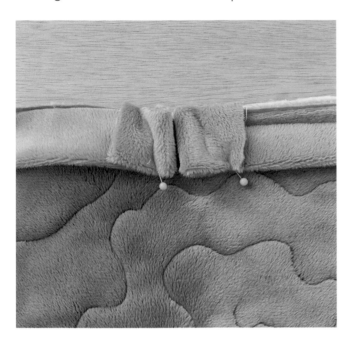

12. Measure 1″ from the fold on each piece of binding. Mark the 1″ and cut.

13. With right sides together, join the ends in the same manner as in Step 3.

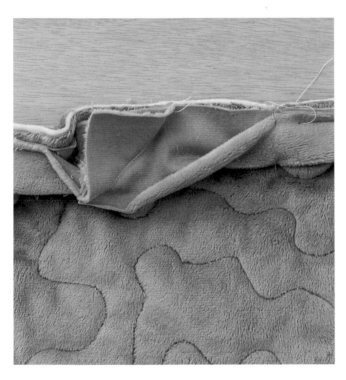

14. Lay the binding flat. Finish sewing to the edge.

15. Turn the binding to the back of the project and hand stitch it down, using a small blind stitch.

NONTRADITIONAL BINDING

There are multiple easy, raw-edge ways to bind with minky cuddle.

Blunt-Edge Style

1. Make the back of the project about 3″ larger on all sides.

2. Quilt as desired.

3. Trim the outer backing to 1″ larger on all sides.

4. Fold the edges in to encase the edges of the quilt. Stitch along the edge. When approaching a corner, stitch to the edge and stop. Bring the next edge over and start stitching from the edge. Continue in this manner.

Contrasting Blunt-Edge Style

1. Cut strips 2″ × width of fabric. (The number of strips is indicated in the project instructions.)

2. Follow Traditional Binding, Steps 2–4 (page 10).

3. Using a single layer, stitch the strips to the back of the project, right sides together. (Unlike in Traditional Binding, there is no need to fold the strips wrong sides together; you will use them as a single thickness.)

4. Continue sewing the binding, following the directions for Traditional Binding, Steps 6–10 (page 10).

5. Fold the edges at a 45° angle and cut ¼″ from the fold. Carefully pin along the fold to mark it and hold together the edges.

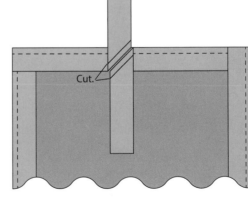

6. Stitch on the fold. Finish sewing the binding to the edge.

7. Bring the binding to the front and stitch along the edge, mitering the corners. Use a serpentine stitch on the front edge.

hatchlings

Finished sizes (wide × tall × deep):

EGG: 5″ × 5½″ × 5″   CHICK: 4″ × 3″ × 4″   ROBIN: 3½″ × 3″ × 5″   SNAKE: 1¾″ × 16″ × 1¼″

Making soft toys for children has many benefits. One major benefit is that these toys don't make noise. If you're in a place where children are supposed to be quiet, just hand them one of these simple toys to play with. You can choose to make a chick, robin, snake—or all three! For small children, use embroidery instead of buttons for the eyes.

materials

EGG

Minky cuddle: ¼ yard white (for Chick), blue (for Robin), or beige (for Snake)

Quilting cotton: ¼ yard for lining for each

Zipper: Nylon, at least 10″ long

CHICK

Yellow minky cuddle: ¼ yard

Felted wool or felt: For beak and feet

Polyester stuffing

Buttons: 2, for eyes

ROBIN

Minky cuddle:

• **Brown:** ⅛ yard

• **Red:** ⅛ yard

Felted wool or felt: For beak and feet

Polyester stuffing

Buttons: 2, for eyes

SNAKE

Green minky cuddle: ⅛ yard

Crushed walnut shells: For stuffing

Buttons: 2, for eyes

cutting

• Download and print the Hatchlings patterns. (For downloading instructions, see Some Essentials for This Book, page 8.)

• Make templates from the patterns. Transfer all markings to the templates.

EGG

Minky cuddle

• Cut 3 of Egg Side.

• Cut 2 of Egg Front (1 and 1 reversed).

Cotton

• Cut 3 of Egg Side.

• Cut 2 of Egg Front (1 and 1 reversed).

• Cut 2 squares 2½″ × 2½″ for zipper.

SNAKE

Green minky cuddle

• Cut 1 of Snake Head Top.

• Cut 1 of Snake Head Bottom.

• Cut 2 strips 2″ × 13″.

CHICK OR ROBIN

Minky cuddle

Use yellow minky cuddle for the Chick. Use brown and red minky cuddle for the Robin, referring to the photo (previous page) for placement.

• Cut 2 of Chick/Robin Side.

• Cut 1 of Chick/Robin Belly.

• Cut 1 of Chick/Robin Top.

• Cut 2 of Chick/Robin Tail.

• Cut 4 of Chick/Robin Wing.

Felted wool or felt

• Cut 2 of Chick/Robin Foot.

• Cut of 1 Chick/Robin Beak.

---

make the egg

All seam allowances are ⅜″ unless otherwise noted.

Prepare the Zipper

1. With the zipper closed, measure 7½″ from the tab end of the zipper tape and mark. Cut the zipper at the mark.

2. Fold 2 edges of the cotton squares 2½″ × 2½″ in toward the center until the edges meet. Press.

3. Place the ends of the zipper inside the folded squares. Stitch across the folded edges, catching the zipper and all layers of the fabric. Trim the edges of the fabric even with the edges of the zipper tape. Repeat for the other end.

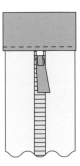

Sew the Zipper to the Egg Front

1. With the tab end at the top, sandwich the left half of the zipper between a minky cuddle Egg Front piece and a lining Egg Front piece, right sides together. Align the straight edges and hand baste or pin securely.

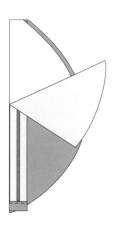

2. Using a zipper foot, stitch through all the layers using a ¼˝ seam allowance.

3. Turn right sides out and lightly press with a pressing stick.

4. Sandwich the right half of the zipper between the other minky cuddle Egg Front and lining Egg Front pieces, right sides together. Align the straight edges and hand baste or pin securely.

5. Stitch through all the layers.

6. Turn right side out.

Sew the Egg Sides

1. Stitch 2 minky cuddle Egg Side pieces right sides together, matching the top edges and sides, and starting and stopping at the marks.

2. Repeat for the third minky cuddle Egg Side piece.

3. Repeat for the lining pieces, leaving a 2˝ opening in one of the seams.

Leave open.

4. Open the zipper, leaving about 1˝ at the bottom zipped.

5. With right sides together, stitch the minky cuddle Egg Front to the minky cuddle Egg Sides. Make sure not to catch the lining.

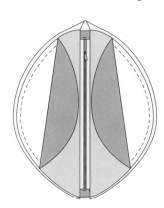

6. With right sides together, sew the lining Egg Front piece to the lining Egg Side piece. Pull the pieces through the opening in the lining side seam. Turn the lining to the inside through the zipper. Mold and shape the egg until the lining fits well inside the egg. Hand stitch the opening in the lining.

make the chick/robin

1. With right sides together, sew together 2 Chick/Robin Wing pieces. Cut a small slit in each wing piece for turning right sides out.

2. With right sides together, sew together the Chick/Robin Tail pieces, leaving a side of the triangle open for turning. Turn right sides out and stitch the open end closed.

3. Stitch the 2 side pieces to the top piece, right sides together, stopping at the mark. Sew the belly to the 2 side pieces, right sides together, leaving an opening for turning right sides out.

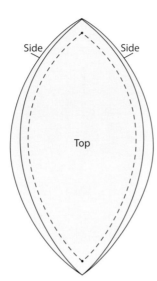

4. Turn the Chick/Robin right sides out. Stuff with polyester stuffing until it has a rounded shape. Hand sew the wings to the sides, making certain that the slit used to turn the wing right side out is against the body and enclosed by the stitching.

5. Hand stitch the tail to the back of the Chick/Robin.

6. Glue the beak to the front of the Chick/Robin where all seams meet. Glue the feet to the bottom of the chick.

7. Attach the button eyes at the marks.

make the snake

1. Stitch a dart in the Snake Head Top.

2. Stitch the Snake Head Top to the Snake Head Bottom, right sides together. Turn the head right sides out.

3. Using scissors, taper the ends of the 2″ × 13″ strips so that they come to a point to form the snake body. Stitch the strips right sides together, leaving a 2″ opening on one side, and leaving the untapered side of the strips open.

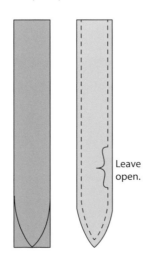

Leave open.

4. Leaving the snake body wrong sides out, slip the head into the body, aligning the side seams of the body with the side seams of the head. Ease to fit. Stitch the head to the body either by machine or by hand.

(tip) *You can sew the seam joining the body to the head with a sewing machine, but it is tricky because the opening is small. Instead, sew this by hand using small stitches.*

5. Turn the snake right sides out through the opening in the side. Pour walnut shells as stuffing through the opening until the snake is full.

6. Hand stitch the opening in the side closed.

7. Attach the button eyes at the marks.

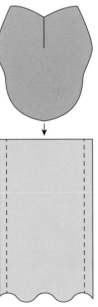

bundle me up stroller wrap

• **Finished size:** 23″ × 43″ •

How many times have you taken a blanket- or quilt-wrapped tot in a stroller on a chilly day, only to have the blanket get caught in the stroller wheels? Or maybe the baby is covered in the front, but the backs of his or her legs are freezing off! This stroller wrap makes it possible for a little one to ride in style and warmth.

materials

Minky cuddle:

• **Main color:** 2 yards

• **Coordinating color:** 2 yards for lining

Coordinating cotton or flannel: 1 yard for bias tape

Woven interfacing or muslin: ½ yard

Quilt batting: Low loft, twin size

Hook-and-loop tape: ¾″ wide, sew-in, 1¼ yards

Separating zippers: 2, each 37″ long

Elastic: 1″ wide, 7½″ long

Quilter's safety pins

D-ring

cutting

• Download and print the Bundle Me Up Stroller Wrap patterns. (For downloading instructions, see Some Essentials for This Book, page 8.)

• Make templates from the patterns. Transfer all markings to the templates.

MAIN-COLOR MINKY CUDDLE

• Cut 1 of Stroller Wrap Front.

• Cut 1 of Stroller Wrap Back—Top.

• Cut 1 of Stroller Wrap Back—Bottom.

• Cut 3 large rectangles 5″ × 8″.

COORDINATING-COLOR MINKY CUDDLE

• Cut 1 of Stroller Wrap Front.

• Cut 1 of Stroller Wrap Back—Top.

• Cut 1 of Stroller Wrap Back—Bottom.

• Cut 3 large rectangles 5″ × 8″.

• Cut 2 small rectangles 3½″ × 6″.

COORDINATING COTTON OR FLANNEL

• Cut 6 bias strips 2½″ wide. Start in the center of the fabric and work outward to yield the longest strips.

NOTE: The bias strips will all be different lengths as you cut from the center of the fabric outward. You will join these to make longer strips as needed. Use the longest ones for the edges of the zippers.

WOVEN INTERFACING OR MUSLIN

• Cut 3 rectangles 5″ × 8″.

QUILT BATTING

• Cut 1 of Stroller Wrap Front.

• Cut 1 of Stroller Wrap Back—Top.

• Cut 1 of Stroller Wrap Back—Bottom.

HOOK-AND-LOOP TAPE

• Cut 1 piece 14½″ long (loop side).

• Cut 1 piece 8″ long (hook side).

• Cut 12 pieces 1½″ long (hook side).

• Cut 2 pieces 12″ long (loop side).

make bias tape

1. Square the ends of the bias strips. Join the bias strips end to end, right sides together, by laying them perpendicular to each other and stitching at a 45° angle from the upper left to lower right. Refer to Traditional Binding, Step 3 (page 10).

2. Trim the corners and press the seams open.

3. Fold the long edges of the bias strips toward the center of the strip so that they meet. Press. Set aside.

prepare the zippers

1. Open the folds on one end of the bias tape. Fold the short end under ½˝, then refold the long edges inward. Press.

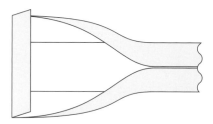

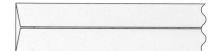

2. Refer to Zipper Anatomy (page 9) and mark "R" and "L" on the right and left halves of the zipper tape. Repeat for both zippers.

3. Starting at the top of the zipper tape, wrap the right half of the zipper with the bias tape, with the folds of the bias tape at the center of the zipper tape. Make sure that the folds are at least ¼˝ away from the zipper teeth. Pin the bias tape all the way to the end of the zipper.

4. Cut the bias strip ½˝ beyond the end of the zipper tape.

5. Remove a few pins to open the folds on the end of the bias tape. Fold the short end under ½˝, then refold the long edges inward as in Step 1. Pin to the end of the zipper.

6. Using a zipper foot, stitch the bias tape onto the zipper through all layers. Backstitch at the beginning and end.

tip *It may help to unzip the zipper about 3˝ before stitching. With the needle down, as you approach the tab, raise the presser foot and zip the zipper closed.*

7. Repeat for the opposite half of the zipper. The zipper is now enclosed on both halves with bias tape.

8. Repeat this process to enclose the second zipper's halves with bias tape.

make the stroller wrap front

All seam allowances are ⅜″ unless otherwise noted.

1. Lay a right zipper half face down on the main-color minky cuddle Stroller Wrap Front left side, matching the markings on the pattern and aligning the edge of the bias tape to the edge of the Stroller Wrap Front. Hand baste or pin securely into place.

2. Repeat Step 1, this time laying a *left* zipper half face down on the Stroller Wrap Front *right* side.

prepare and attach the lining

All seam allowances are ⅜″ unless otherwise noted.

1. Layer the Stroller Wrap Front quilt batting with the wrong side of the Stroller Wrap Front lining. Machine baste ¼″ in from the edges.

2. Lay the Stroller Wrap Front lining and main-color minky cuddle Stroller Wrap Front right sides together. Pin securely. Stitch through all layers, leaving a small 2″ opening above the zipper on one side for turning right sides out.

3. Turn right sides out and stitch the opening closed.

make the stroller wrap back

Join the Stroller Wrap Back Top and Bottom

1. With right sides together, stitch the main-color minky cuddle Stroller Wrap Back—Bottom to the Stroller Wrap Back—Top.

2. Repeat for the Stroller Wrap Back—Top and the Stroller Wrap Back—Bottom lining pieces.

3. Sew the darts in the Stroller Wrap Back—Bottom on both the back and the lining pieces.

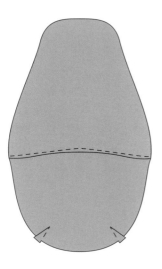

Make the Back Strap

1. Cut a 22″ piece of bias tape. Open the folds on one end of the bias tape. Fold the short end under ½″, then refold the long edges inward. Press.

2. Stitch a 14½″ loop-side piece of hook-and-loop tape to the wrong side.

3. On the same piece of bias tape, stitch an 8″ hook-side piece of hook-and-loop tape. Slightly overlap the piece onto the loop-side piece.

←—14½″ Loop side —→ ← 8″ Hook side →

4. Stitch a D-ring to an end of the elastic.

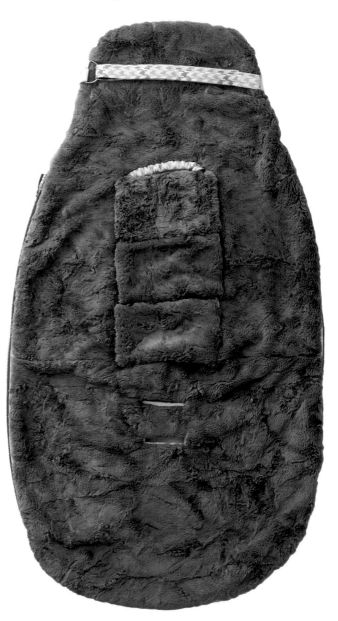

Make the Large Rectangle Back Sections

1. Stitch 4 of the 1½″ hook side pieces of hook-and-loop tape to the right side of the coordinating color large rectangles, ½″ in from the edges. Repeat for the other 2 rectangles.

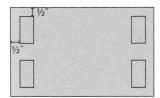

2. Reinforce the wrong side of the rectangles with interfacing. Either use a pressing cloth and fuse the interfacing (if fusible), or stitch using a scant ¼″ seam allowance.

3. Lay a main-color minky cuddle large rectangle right sides together with a coordinating-color minky cuddle large rectangle.

4. Stitch a ⅜″ seam allowance around the rectangle, leaving a 2″ opening for turning right sides out.

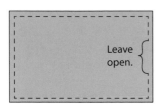

Leave open.

5. Turn right sides out and stitch the opening closed. Repeat for a total of 3 rectangles.

Sew the Zipper

1. Pin the end of the elastic without the D-ring to the right side of the Stroller Wrap Back lining, as shown.

2. Pin the end of the bias tape with the hook-and-loop tape to the right side of the Stroller Wrap Back lining, as shown, with the hook-and-loop tape facing up.

3. Refer to Make the Stroller Wrap Front (page 19) to insert and sew in the second zipper, following the markings on the pattern.

(tip) *Make sure that you sew the corresponding zipper half to the correct side of the Stroller Wrap Back. It is a good idea to actually zip together the zippers first so that you know which one goes on the right side of the Stroller Wrap Back and which one goes on the left side of the Stroller Wrap Back.*

4. Lay the main-color minky cuddle and lining Stroller Wrap Back pieces right sides together. Stitch through all the layers, making sure to catch the ends of the elastic and bias tape pieces and the zippers. Leave a 2½″ opening at the top for turning.

5. Turn right sides out. Hand stitch the opening closed.

Make the Stroller Strap Opening

1. Using quilter's safety pins, pin through all the layers of the Stroller Wrap Back pieces to keep any of the layers from shifting. It is important that they remain stationary for accurate cutting.

2. Using the Stroller Strap Cutout template, mark the cutout using a washable fabric marker on the lining side. Stitch on the line through all layers.

3. Cut ¼″ inside the stitching, cutting a hole in the Stroller Wrap Back layers. Discard the cut-out piece.

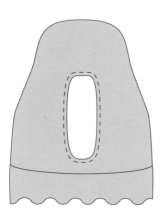

4. Using 40″ of bias tape, open the folds on 1 side. Stitch the open side of the bias tape to the cut-out edge of the lining piece. Stitch inside the fold and ease at the corners. Overlap the ends.

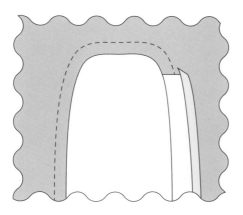

5. Turn the bias tape to the main-color minky cuddle side of the Stroller Wrap Back. Hand stitch the folded edge to the Stroller Wrap Back, using a small blind stitch.

6. On the main-color minky cuddle side of the Stroller Wrap Back, stitch 2 pieces 12″ long of hook-and-loop fastener, loop-side, to the long sides of the opening, partially covering the bias tape.

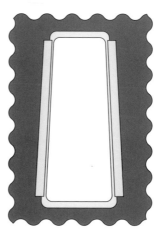

Make the Buckle Openings

1. On the wrong side of the coordinating-color minky cuddle small rectangles, mark a rectangle 3¼″ × ½″ in the center.

2. Lay the small rectangle pieces over the markings on the Stroller Wrap Back, right sides together.

3. Stitch directly on the marked rectangle.

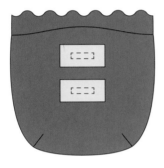

4. Cut the rectangle open, clipping the corners.

5. Turn the small rectangles to the inside, pulling firmly. Pin.

6. Turn the edges under ¼″. Using a small blind stitch, hand stitch around the rectangle.

Tuck in the little tot to stay warm!

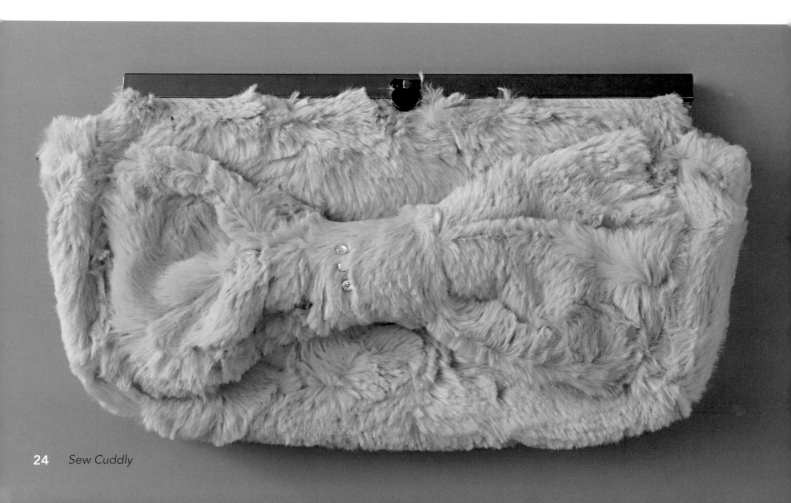

cuddle clutch purse

• **Finished size:** 12″ wide × 7″ high × 3½″ deep •

This elegant little clutch is perfect for a night out, or whenever a large purse won't fit the bill. Make it for a winter wedding or Valentine's Day. This project offers two exterior embellishment options: the bow (see Embellish the Purse Front, page 29) or the horseshoes (see Alternative Embellishment: Horseshoes, page 29).

materials

Minky cuddle: ⅜ yard

Quilting cotton: ½ yard for lining

Fusible woven interfacing: ½ yard

Heavyweight stabilizer: Firm, ⅛″ thick, ⅛ yard

Faux suede or leather (*optional*): ¼ yard for appliqué

Sticky stabilizer (*optional*): Such as Wash-Away Stitch Stabilizer (by C&T Publishing) or Sulky Sticky Fabri-Solvy Stabilizer, ¼ yard for appliqué

Zippers: 2 nylon, 22″ long and 12″ long

Purse clasp closure: 10″ wide

Heat-set rhinestones with setting tool

(tip) I prefer fusible woven interfacings or fusible, muslin-like interfacings over nonwovens. They give much more body and stability to bags and garments and are often easier to work with, especially where ironing is concerned.

cutting

• Download and print the Cuddle Clutch Purse patterns. (For downloading instructions, see Some Essentials for This Book, page 8.)

• Make templates from the patterns. Transfer all markings to the templates.

(tip) If you're embellishing the exterior of the purse with an appliqué, such as the provided horseshoes appliqué, refer to Alternative Embellishment: Horseshoes (page 29) prior to beginning the project.

MINKY CUDDLE

• Cut 1 of Exterior Rectangle 10½″ × 14″.

• Cut 1 of Bow Rectangle 10½″ × 8½″.

• Cut 1 of Bow Knot Rectangle 3½″ × 4″.

• Cut 2 of Side Wedge.

QUILTING COTTON

• Cut 1 of Purse Lining Rectangle 10½″ × 14″.

• Cut 2 of Center Pocket Rectangle 9½″ × 10½″.

• Cut 2 of Inset Pocket Rectangle 9½″ × 4″.

• Cut 2 of Purse Lining Wedge.

FUSIBLE WOVEN INTERFACING

• Cut 1 rectangle 10½″ × 14″.

• Cut 1 rectangle 9½″ × 10½″.

HEAVYWEIGHT STABILIZER

• Cut 2 strips 10″ × ⅜″.

make the center pocket

All seam allowances are ⅜˝ unless otherwise noted.

NOTE: Use the 22˝ zipper for the center pocket for ease in construction. Refer to Zipper Anatomy (page 9) and mark "R" and "L" on the right and left halves of the zipper tape.

1. Fuse the interfacing to the wrong side of a Center Pocket Rectangle.

2. Lay the 22˝ zipper front side down on top the interfaced Center Pocket Rectangle, right side up, lining up the left half of the zipper with the 10½˝ edge.

3. Lay the second Center Pocket Rectangle over the zipper, right sides together with the first Center Pocket Rectangle, aligning the 10½˝ edge with the left half of the zipper. Hand baste or pin securely.

4. Using a zipper foot, stitch through all 3 layers with a ¼˝ seam, catching the left half of the zipper.

5. Turn the fabric and the right half of the zipper right sides out. Press.

6. Separately, fold both rectangles right sides together and align with the edge of the right half of the zipper. Hand baste or pin securely.

7. Stitch through all 3 layers.

8. Turn the entire pocket unit right sides out. Unzip the zipper and press the seams flat next to the zipper.

9. Close the zipper and press a crease at the bottom of the pocket to mark the center bottom.

assemble the lining and inset pockets

1. Fuse the interfacing to the Purse Lining Rectangle. Fold in half and mark the center of the 14″ sides.

2. Measuring 1″ from a long edge, center and mark a ½″ × 7½″ rectangle on an Inset Pocket rectangle.

3. Lay the Inset Pocket Rectangle right sides together with the Purse Lining, centered and ¾″ from the top edge.

4. Stitch directly on the lines drawn on the Inset Pocket Rectangle.

5. Cut a slit in the center of the stitching. Clip the corners.

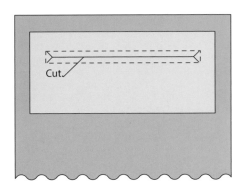

6. Pull the Inset Pocket Rectangle through the stitching so that the wrong sides are together. Press flat.

7. Lay the shorter zipper under the opening so that the tab is at an end of the opening, and the zipper shows through the middle of the opening. Hand baste or pin the zipper in place securely.

8. Using a zipper foot, stitch the zipper into place by stitching ¼″ around the entire opening. Cut the zipper length ½″ beyond the stitching.

9. Lay the second Inset Pocket Rectangle right sides together with the first Inset Pocket Rectangle.

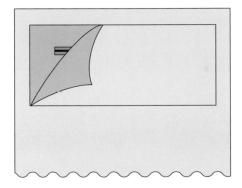

10. Without catching the purse lining, stitch the rectangles together with a ¼″ seam around the entire perimeter.

insert the center pocket

1. With the 22″ zipper unzipped, match the Center Pocket crease with the center markings on the lining. Pin the Center Pocket to the lining along the crease.

2. Stitch the Center Pocket to the lining through all the layers.

3. Pull the zipper closed. Cut the zipper even with the end of the Center Pocket.

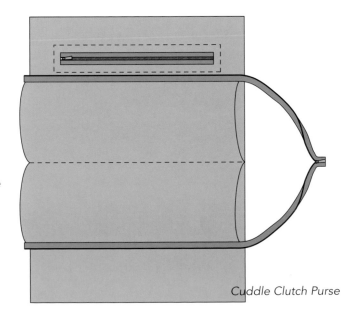

assemble the lining sides

1. Match the center markings on each Cotton Lining Wedge with the Center Pocket. Stitch each wedge to the lining, right sides together, using a generous ¼″ seam, catching the bottom of the Center Pocket.

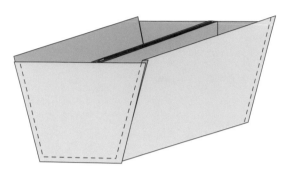

2. Pinch the Center Pocket between the lines marked on the Cotton Lining Wedge. Pin along the lines.

3. Stitch along the lines, starting at the top end of the Center Pocket and backstitching ½″. Make certain to catch and enclose the ends of the Center Pocket and the zipper.

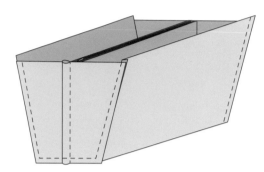

4. Repeat Steps 1–3 for the second Cotton Lining Wedge.

---

make the purse exterior

With right sides together, stitch the minky cuddle Purse Side Wedges to the minky cuddle Exterior Rectangle, matching center markings.

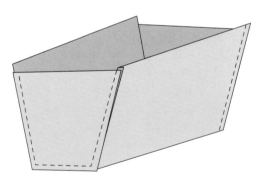

Sew the Lining to the Exterior

1. With right sides together, pin the Cotton Lining Wedges to the minky cuddle Purse Side Wedges along the top exposed edge.

2. Pin the sides of the lining rectangle to the sides of the minky cuddle Exterior rectangle, leaving the 10½″ edges of the rectangle open for turning.

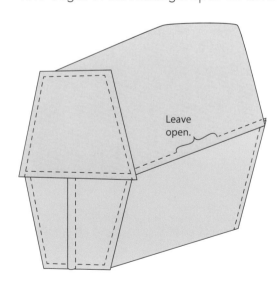

Leave open.

3. Stitch. Turn right sides out.

4. Shape the purse so that the lining fits smoothly down into the exterior.

attach the purse clasps

Note: If your purse clasp includes instructions, follow them along with the instructions below.

1. Using a wooden skewer or a flat head screwdriver, push the 10½˝ edge of the purse into the purse clasp that has the hinged tab. The hinged tab should be on the lining side of the purse.

2. Apply a fine line of glue to a heavyweight stabilizer strip, and push this into the purse clasp over the edge of the purse already inserted. Fasten with the screws provided with the clasp.

3. Cut a small notch in the center of the opposite side of the purse top, ⅝˝ wide and ¼˝ deep.

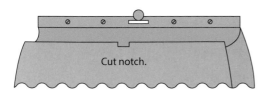

Cut notch.

4. Repeat Steps 1 and 2 for the opposite side of the purse.

embellish the purse front

1. Fold the Bow Rectangle in half lengthwise, right sides together. Stitch the edges, leaving a 2˝ opening.

2. Turn right sides out. Hand stitch the opening closed.

3. Fold the Bow Knot Rectangle in half lengthwise, right sides together. Stitch the long edge, leaving the 2 short edges open for turning.

4. Turn right sides out.

5. Pleat the center of the Bow Rectangle. Wrap the Bow Knot Rectangle around the Bow Rectangle. Hand stitch the ends.

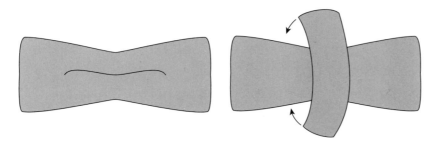

6. Embellish with heat-set rhinestones, referring to the manufacturer's directions.

ALTERNATIVE EMBELLISHMENT
Horseshoes

1. Apply sticky stabilizer to faux suede or leather.

2. Transfer the pattern for the Horseshoe Appliqué onto the sticky stabilizer.

3. Cut out the horseshoes.

4. Peel the sticky stabilizer and adhere to the clutch exterior as desired.

5. Use your preferred machine appliqué stitch to sew the horseshoes to the purse exterior.

6. Embellish with heat-set rhinestones, referring to the manufacturer's directions.

animal hats

● **Finished size:** 8″ wide × 8″ tall × 8″ deep ●

These hats are not only warm but a fun fashion accessory. There are small, medium, and large versions, so even an adult can have fun with these.

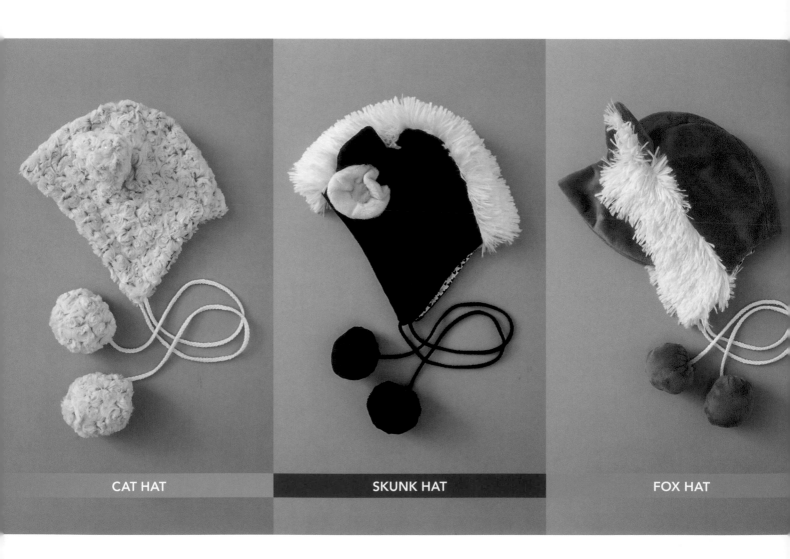

CAT HAT

SKUNK HAT

FOX HAT

materials

CAT HAT

Minky cuddle: ⅓ yard

Quilting cotton: ½ yard for lining

Cotton cording: 1 yard

Polyester stuffing

SKUNK HAT

Minky cuddle:

• **Black:** ⅓ yard

• **White shaggy:** ¼ yard for hat center

• **White:** Small piece at least 6″ × 6″ for flower

• **Yellow:** Small piece for flower center

Quilting cotton: ½ yard for lining

Cotton cording: 1 yard

FOX HAT

Minky cuddle:

• **Rust colored:** ⅓ yard

• **White shaggy:** ¼ yard for hat center

Quilting cotton: ½ yard for lining

Fusible woven interfacing: ¼ yard

Cotton cording: 1 yard

cutting

• Download and print the Animal Hats patterns. (For downloading instructions, see Some Essentials for This Book, page 8.)

• Make templates from the patterns. Transfer all markings to the templates.

CAT HAT

Minky cuddle

• Cut 2 of Hat Side (1 and 1 reversed).

• Cut 2 of Front Hat Side (1 and 1 reversed).

• Cut 1 of Hat Center.

• Cut 4 of Ear.

• Cut 2 of Pom-Pom.

Quilting cotton

• Cut 1 of Hat Center for lining.

• Cut 2 of Hat Side Lining (1 and 1 reversed).

SKUNK HAT

Black minky cuddle

• Cut 2 of Hat Side (1 and 1 reversed).

• Cut 2 of Front Hat Side (1 and 1 reversed).

• Cut 4 of Ear.

White shaggy minky cuddle

• Cut 1 of Hat Center.

White minky cuddle

• Cut 2 of Flower Circle.

Yellow minky cuddle

• Cut 1 of Flower Center.

Quilting cotton

• Cut 1 of Hat Center for lining.

• Cut 2 of Hat Side Lining (1 and 1 reversed).

FOX HAT

Rust minky cuddle

• Cut 2 of Hat Brim.

• Cut 2 of Hat Side (1 and 1 reversed).

• Cut 1 of Hat Center.

• Cut 4 of Ear.

• Cut 2 of Pom-Pom.

White shaggy minky cuddle

• Cut 2 of Front Hat Side (1 and 1 reversed).

• Cut 2 of Small Ear Triangle.

Quilting cotton

• Cut 1 of Hat Center for lining.

• Cut 2 of Hat Side Lining (1 and 1 reversed).

Woven interfacing

• Cut 1 of Hat Brim.

cat hat   *All seam allowances are ⅜˝ unless otherwise noted.*

Make the Ears

1. With right sides together, sew 2 Cat Ear sections together along the top 2 sides.

2. Stuff with polyester stuffing to your desired thickness. Set aside.

Make the Hat

1. Position the Ears onto the Hat Sides, according to the markings. Baste in place by machine or by hand.

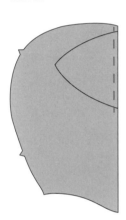

2. With right sides together, pin the Front Hat Side to the Hat Side, matching the notches. Stitch.

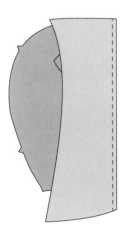

3. Repeat Step 2 for the opposite side.

4. Pin the Hat Center to both the left and the right Hat Sides, matching the notches. Stitch.

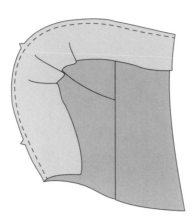

Make the Lining

1. Stitch the Hat Side Lining to the Hat Center Lining, right sides together, matching notches.

2. Press the seams toward the Hat Center.

Join the Lining to the Hat

1. Cut the cotton cording in half. Stitch to the right side of the minky cuddle on the Front Hat Side where marked.

2. With right sides together, stitch the Hat Lining to the Hat, leaving a 2˝ opening at the neck edge of the Hat Center for turning right sides out.

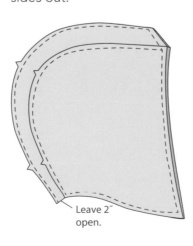

Leave 2˝ open.

3. Turn right side out. Stitch the opening closed by hand, using an small blind stitch.

Make the Pom-Poms

1. With a hand-stitching needle and doubled thread, make a running stitch around the Pom-Pom piece about ½˝ in from the edges. Pull the thread, gathering the Pom-Pom. Leave an opening and fill with polyester stuffing.

2. When the Pom-Pom is stuffed full, pull the stitching tight. Insert the end of the cotton cording about 1˝ into the Pom-Pom, catching it as you hand stitch the Pom-Pom closed. Knot.

3. Repeat Steps 1 and 2 for the second Pom-Pom.

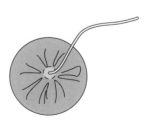

skunk hat

All seam allowances are ⅜″ unless otherwise noted.

1. With right sides together, stitch the Ears.

2. Following the placement markings, baste half of the Ear to the Front Hat Side. Repeat for the opposite side.

3. With right sides together, stitch the Hat Side to the Front Hat Side for both sides of the hat, catching the basted half of the Ear in the seam.

4. Baste the free half of the Ear to the top of the Front Hat Side for both sides of the hat.

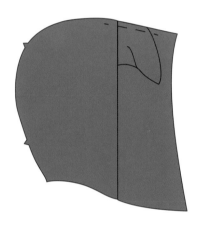

5. With right sides together and matching notches, stitch the Hat Center to the Front Hat Side/Hat Side unit, catching the other half of the Ear into the seam. Repeat for the opposite side.

6. Follow the Cat Hat instructions (previous page) for Make the Lining, Join the Lining to the Hat, and Make the Pom-Poms.

Flower

1. Stitch 2 Flower Circles right sides together. Cut a small slit in one side of the flower for turning right sides out.

2. Turn right sides out. Stitch the small slit closed by hand.

3. Appliqué the Flower Center to the middle of the flower on the side without the slit.

4. Using a large running stitch, stitch around the Flower Center. Gather the flower by pulling the stitching and making a knot.

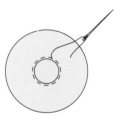

5. Hand stitch the flower to the hat with the slit side against the hat.

---

fox hat

All seam allowances are ⅜″ unless otherwise noted.

1. Appliqué the Small Ear Triangles to the Ears.

2. Follow Skunk Hat, Steps 1–5 (above) for the ears.

3. Apply fusible woven interfacing to a Hat Brim piece, using low heat on the iron and following the manufacturer's directions.

4. With right sides together, stitch the outside edge of the Hat Brim, leaving the hat side of the Hat Brim open.

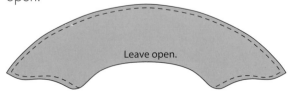

Leave open.

5. Turn right sides out.

6. Stitch the Hat Brim to the hat, matching the center of the Hat Brim to the middle of the Hat Center. Keep the hat brim against the hat.

7. Follow the Cat Hat instructions (previous page) for Make the Lining, Join the Lining to the Hat, and Make the Pom-Poms.

gauntlets

• **Finished size:** 6″ × 9″ •

If you live in a cold climate, you know that fashion and warmth aren't always in lockstep, especially when we need to use our electronics. Even in warmer climates, there are cooler mornings and evenings when you need just a touch of something to keep you warm. These gauntlets are perfect for these occasions. Soft and warm, they are quick to sew up, and look so attractive. Embellish them with a pretty vintage button, and you're sure to want to make more than one pair.

NOTE: When cutting pattern pieces, you need mirror images of each other. Make sure to either cut the fabric right sides together, or, if the fabric is too thick and you need to cut them one at a time, flip over the pattern piece or the fabric. The pieces must mirror each other.

materials

Minky cuddle:

• **Main color:** ¼ yard

• **Accent color:** ¼ yard

Jersey knit to match minky cuddle:
¼ yard for lining

Buttons: 2

Thread to match

cutting

• Download and print the Gauntlets patterns. (For downloading instructions, see Some Essentials for This Book, page 8.)

• Make templates from the patterns. Transfer all markings to the templates.

MAIN-COLOR MINKY CUDDLE

• Cut 2 of Gauntlet Sleeve (1 and 1 reversed).

• Cut 2 rectangles 10″ × 2½″ for top bands.

ACCENT-COLOR MINKY CUDDLE

• Cut 2 of Gauntlet Top (1 and 1 reversed).

• Cut 2 of Gauntlet Thumb (1 and 1 reversed).

JERSEY KNIT

• Cut 2 of Gauntlet Thumb (1 and 1 reversed).

• Cut 2 of Gauntlet Top (1 and 1 reversed).

• Cut 2 of Gauntlet Sleeve (1 and 1 reversed).

assemble the gauntlet

All seam allowances are ⅜″ unless otherwise noted.

1. With right sides together, pin the minky cuddle Gauntlet Thumb to the minky cuddle Gauntlet Top. Stitch the seam, easing the curves.

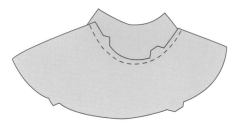

2. Stitch the minky cuddle Gauntlet Thumb seam, right sides together, stopping at the seamline of the minky cuddle Gauntlet Top.

3. With right sides together, stitch the minky cuddle Gauntlet Top to the minky cuddle Gauntlet Sleeve.

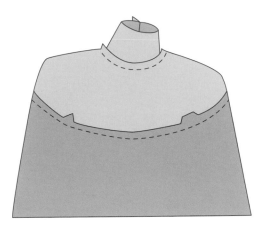

4. With right sides together, stitch the center seam.

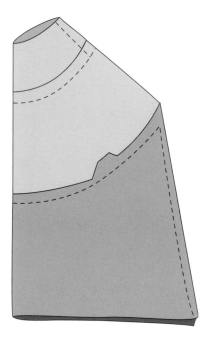

make the lining

Using the jersey knit pieces, follow directions for Assemble the Gauntlet, Steps 1–4 (previous page).

apply the lining

(tip) When adding the lining, it is a good idea to put the gauntlet onto your hand, right side out, to make certain that you have the correct lining for the correct gauntlet. Put the lining over it, wrong side out, right sides together with the gauntlet. The lining's right side should be a mirror image of the gauntlet's right side. Make sure that the seams align.

1. With right sides together, slip the gauntlet inside the gauntlet lining. Stitch around the top of the thumb opening, making certain to catch both layers.

2. Bring the lining to the inside of the gauntlet through the thumb.

3. Arrange the lining to fit well inside the gauntlet.

make the band

1. Fold the band lengthwise, right sides together. Stitch the short ends, leaving the long end open. Turn right sides out.

2. Using a long stitch on the sewing machine, or using hand basting, baste the lining to the Gauntlet Top.

3. Position the end of the band on the Gauntlet Top in a spot that is pleasing to your eye, at least 1″ from the center seam. It can go from left to right, or right to left,

but the end of the band should be on the front of the gauntlet, and the bands should be mirror images of each other.

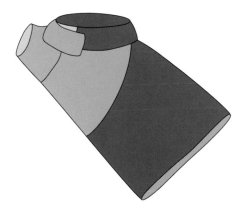

4. Baste or pin the band securely to the top of the gauntlet. The edges of the band will overlap.

5. Making certain to catch the lining and gauntlet, stitch the band to the Gauntlet Top through all layers.

6. Finish the seam with a close zigzag stitch or serger.

7. Sew a decorative button to the end of the band.

finish the lining

1. Turn the edge of the Gauntlet Sleeve under ¼″, right side to wrong side. Turn the lining Gauntlet Sleeve under ¼″, right side to wrong side.

2. Align the Gauntlet Sleeve with the lining. Stitch together the pieces, using a small blind stitch.

NOTE: You may need to ease the lining slightly to fit the sleeve, as the jersey may have stretched during the process.

reading pillow

• **Finished size:** 33″ wide × 17″ long × 20″ deep •

Have you ever taken a book to bed only to find that you don't get enough support behind your back and arms? It's difficult to read in bed without one of these pillows. Every bookworm in your family will want one!

tip There is a pivot point at the bottom of the Reading Pillow Front that can be slightly confusing if not worked with plain fabric first. It is helpful to make this using muslin first so that you get a feel for where you need to pivot.

materials

Alpaca minky cuddle: 1½ yard

Polyester stuffing: 3 large bags (24 ounces each)

Thread to match

cutting

• Download and print the Reading Pillow patterns. (For downloading instructions, see Some Essentials for This Book, page 8.)

• Make templates from the patterns. Transfer all markings to the templates.

ALPACA MINKY CUDDLE

• Cut 1 of Reading Pillow Front.

• Cut 2 of Reading Pillow Arm.

• Cut 2 strips 28½″ × 2½″ for armbands.

• Cut 1 of Reading Pillow Back.

make the reading pillow

All seam allowances are ⅜″ unless otherwise noted.

1. Transfer all markings from the templates onto the fabric.

2. With right sides together, stitch the armbands to the Reading Pillow Arms along 3 sides, excluding the side with the convex curve.

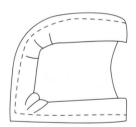

3. Open the bands.

4. Stitch the Reading Pillow Arms with the armbands to the concave curved areas of the Reading Pillow Front, easing along the curves.

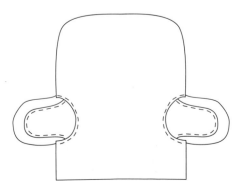

5. With right sides together, hand baste or securely pin the Reading Pillow Back to the Reading Pillow Front, pivoting at the lower corner of the Reading Pillow Front where marked on the pattern.

6. Stitch the Reading Pillow Back to the Reading Pillow Front, pivoting where marked, and leaving a 5″ opening at the base for turning right sides out and stuffing.

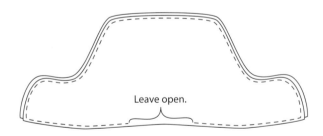

Leave open.

7. Turn right sides out and stuff the pillow with polyester stuffing, making sure it is stuffed very firmly. Stitch the bottom opening closed.

Sit back, relax, and read on!

poncho

• **Finished size:** 59″ × 35″ •

Add warmth and elegance to your fall and winter outerwear. This poncho is one-size-fits-most, and it will make you look like you spent a fortune at an exclusive boutique.

materials

Luxe cuddle: 2 yards

Lining fabric (cotton quilting fabric or satin): 3½ yards

Buttons: 10 decorative

cutting

• Download and print the Poncho patterns. (For downloading instructions, see Some Essentials for This Book, page 8.)

• Make templates from the patterns. Transfer all markings to the templates.

LUXE CUDDLE

• Cut 1 of Poncho Front on fold.

• Cut 1 of Poncho Back on fold.

• Cut 2 rectangles 18″ × 42″ for sleeves.

• Cut 1 rectangle 32″ × 10½″ for cowl.

LINING

• Cut 1 of Poncho Front on fold.

• Cut 1 of Poncho Back on fold.

• Cut 2 rectangles 18″ × 42″ for sleeves.

• Cut 1 strip 2½″ × 34″ on the bias.

make the bias binding strip

Refer to Bundle Me Up Stroller Wrap, Make Bias Tape, Steps 1–3 (page 18), and fold the edges of the 2½″ × 34″ bias strip lengthwise in toward the center of the strip, creating a bias tape. Press.

make the poncho

All seam allowances are ⅜″ unless otherwise noted.

1. With right sides together, stitch the Poncho Front to the Poncho Back along the shoulder seams.

2. Mark the centers of the 42″ sides of the minky cuddle sleeve rectangles.

3. With right sides together, match the center of a minky cuddle sleeve rectangle with a shoulder seam. Pin both sides.

4. Stitch the sleeve to the poncho side. Repeat for the opposite side.

5. Repeat Steps 1–4 for the lining.

6. With right sides together, pin the lining to the poncho along the sides and the sleeves. Leave the neck edge and the bottom edges open.

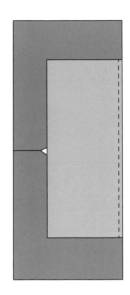

7. Baste or securely pin the poncho to the lining at the sides, the sleeve sides, and the sleeve ends.

8. Stitch the poncho to the lining on the poncho sides, sleeve sides, and sleeve ends. Clip the corners.

9. Turn right sides out through the bottom.

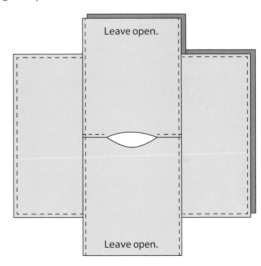

10. Pin the short edges of the cowl rectangle right sides together. Stitch.

11. Fold the cowl wrong sides together.

12. With right sides together, pin securely and baste the raw edges of the cowl to the poncho neck opening, matching the cowl seam with the center back. Ease the cowl and neck edge to fit. Stitch.

13. Stitch the long edge of the bias tape to the cowl seam allowance, overlapping at the beginning and the end.

14. Fold the opposite edge over the seam allowance, encasing the seam allowance, and hand stitch along the fold using a small blind stitch.

Handstitch.

15. Zigzag or serge the bottom edge of the cuddle layer of the poncho. Turn under 1˝ and hem.

16. Repeat Step 15 for the lining, but turn under 1½˝ and hem.

17. Make 5 equally spaced buttonholes, sized according to your button size, on the front lower edge of the sleeve. Stitch the buttons on the inside of the sleeve, equally spaced for the buttonholes. Repeat for the opposite sleeve.

18. Button the sleeves closed.

fox stole

• Finished size: 8˝ × 54˝ •

Do you have a fox or mink stole that belonged to your grandmother? They used to circle the neck and the mouth clipped onto the tail. It looked like it was biting its own tail! Now we have faux fur that looks just like the real thing. Let's make one and let the fun begin.

materials

Luxe cuddle: ½ yard

Polar fleece: ¼ yard

Hook-and-loop tape: Small piece

Buttons: 2, for eyes

Thread to match

cutting

• Download and print the Fox Stole patterns. (For downloading instructions, see Some Essentials for This Book, page 8.)

• Make templates from the patterns. Transfer all markings to the templates.

LUXE CUDDLE

• Cut 4 of Ear.

• Cut 1 of Face.

• Cut 2 of Side Face (1 and 1 reversed).

• Cut 1 of Lower Jaw.

• Cut 2 of Front/Back Neck.

• Cut 2 of Tail.

• Cut 1 strip 14″ × 39″.

POLAR FLEECE

• Cut 2 of Mouth Gusset.

• Cut 1 Nose.

make the head

All seam allowances are ⅜″ unless otherwise noted.

1. With right sides together, stitch the Ears. Turn right sides out.

2. Hand baste the Ears to the upper curved edges of the Face.

3. With right sides together, stitch the Side Face to the Face, catching the Ears, and easing the curves as necessary.

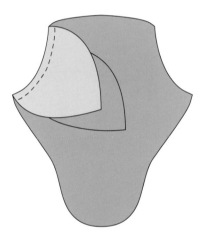

4. Keep the Ears folded down toward the face. Hand baste the curved edge of the Front Neck to the Face, right sides together. Stitch.

5. Stitch the hook-and-loop tape onto the Mouth Gusset pieces where indicated on pattern.

6. With right sides together, stitch a Mouth Gusset to the front of the Face, leaving the edge open as marked on the pattern. Turn right sides out.

7. With right sides together, stitch the other Mouth Gusset to the Lower Jaw, leaving the edge open as marked on the pattern.

8. With right sides together, stitch the curved edge of the Back Neck to the Lower Jaw, being careful not to catch the Mouth Gusset.

9. With right sides together, stitch the Front Neck to the Back Neck, along the sides of the neck, but stopping where marked on the pattern, just beyond the beginning of the Mouth Gusset. Leave the edge open.

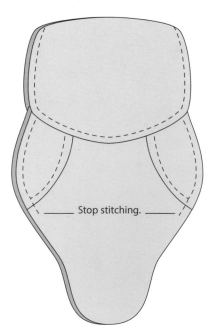

10. Turn right sides out.

11. Pull the Mouth Gusset pieces out through the neck, and stitch them together along the open edges. Push this back in through the neck.

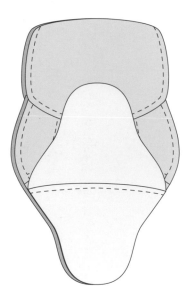

make the body

1. Create a tube by folding the 14″ × 39″ strip right sides together lengthwise and stitching the long edges together. The seam will be on the underside of the fox.

2. Increase the stitch length on the sewing machine and stitch a long stitch around the open end of the tube, then slightly gather it.

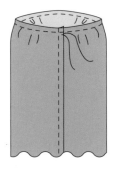

3. Keep the strip wrong side out and slip the completed fox head into the tube, with the right sides together. Make certain the seam of the tube matches with the center underside of the fox neck.

4. Stitch the completed head to the tube at the neck, gathering the tube to fit the head.

5. Turn right sides out.

6. Hand stitch the nose where indicated on the pattern. Attach the button eyes where marked.

make the tail

1. Stitch the 2 Tail pieces right sides together, leaving the end open. Turn right sides out.

2. Increase the stitch length on the sewing machine and stitch a long stitch around the end of the tube, then slightly gather it.

3. Stuff the straight, un-sewn edge of the Tail into the tube. Pull the gathering stitch on the tube to close it around the Tail. Stitch across the end of the tube, securing the Tail.

Drape the stole around your shoulders and catch the tail with the fox's mouth. Enjoy!

bath mat

• **Finished size:** 37″ × 54″ •

This bath mat is generous enough to cover the entire floor in front of the tub. You'll have cozy, warm feet that won't slip when you step out of the tub. You'll also be surprised at how absorbent this wonderful fabric is.

materials

Minky cuddle:

- **6 colors:** ⅓ yard of *each* color

- **White:** ½ yard

- **Chevron or striped:** ¼ yard

Canvas: 60″ wide, 1¼ yards

Stabilizer (such as lightweight interfacing): ½ yard

Cotton quilt batting: Twin size

Adhesive basting spray

Thread to match

cutting

WOF = width of fabric

- Download and print the Bath Mat patterns. (For downloading instructions, see Some Essentials for This Book, page 8.)

- Make templates from the patterns. Transfer all markings to the templates.

ASSORTED-COLORS MINKY CUDDLE

- Cut 1 strip 10″ × 36½″ of *each* color.

WHITE MINKY CUDDLE

- Cut 4 of Large Raindrop.

- Cut 1 of Medium Raindrop.

- Cut 1 of Small Raindrop.

CHEVRON OR STRIPED MINKY CUDDLE

- Cut 4 strips 2½″ × WOF for binding.

CANVAS

- Cut 1 rectangle 36½″ × 54″.

STABILIZER

- Cut 4 of Large Raindrop.

- Cut 1 of Medium Raindrop.

- Cut 1 of Small Raindrop.

QUILT BATTING

- Cut 1 rectangle 36½″ × 54″.

make the raindrops

Layer the stabilizer with the corresponding raindrop. Pin, hand baste, or spray baste them together. Set aside.

prepare the canvas

All seam allowances are ⅜″ unless otherwise noted.

1. Layer the canvas rectangle and the quilt batting rectangle. Hand baste or pin around the edges securely.

2. Find the center of the canvas on a long side. Mark a straight line on the center from one edge of the canvas to the opposite edge.

3. From the centerline, measure 9″ to the right and mark another straight line. Do the same on the left of the centerline.

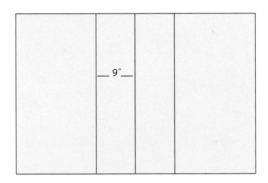

4. Continue to mark lines 9″ apart until you reach the outer sides of the rectangle.

5. Spray adhesive basting spray in the far left 9″ marked space.

6. Lay a 10″ × WOF strip of minky cuddle right side up in this space, smoothing it so that it sticks to the adhesive spray. Hand baste on the edges of the strip through all layers.

7. Lay the next 10″ × WOF strip right sides together with the basted strip. Pin securely along the right-hand edge. Stitch through all the layers.

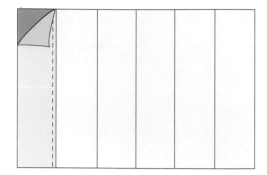

8. Spray the adhesive spray in the next 9″ marked space. Open the second minky cuddle strip, smoothing it so that it sticks to the adhesive spray.

9. Repeat Steps 7 and 8 until all the strips are used and the entire quilt batting is covered.

10. Hand baste the right edge through all the layers.

stitch the raindrops

1. Place the raindrops onto the minky cuddle strips in an arrangement similar to the photo, or design your own arrangement. Pin securely.

2. Using a tight zigzag stitch, appliqué the raindrops to the strips.

finish the bath mat

1. Stitch together the chevron minky cuddle strips end to end along the short ends.

2. Fold the strips wrong sides together lengthwise.

3. Pin the strips onto the edges of the mat, then stitch. (See Traditional Binding, page 10.)

4. Fold the binding to the wrong side of the mat and stitch, using a small blind stitch.

tip *When using this mat, you may want to put a backing on it to prevent it from slipping. There are many commercially prepared products that you can spray or paint onto the canvas to keep it from slipping, or you can use a non-skid rug backing.*

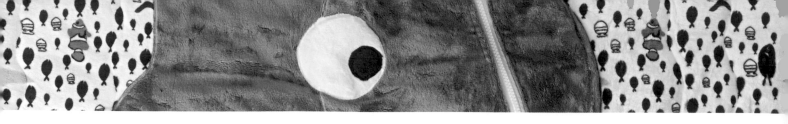

sleep sack

• **Finished size:** 30″ × 60″ •

This sleep sack is great for a sleepover or campout on a not-so-wintry night.
The shark has a mouth big enough to fit pajamas and a toothbrush!

materials

WOF = width of fabric

Minky cuddle:

• **Gray:** ¾ yard

• **White:** ⅛ yard

• **Navy:** ⅛ yard

• **Shark print:** 1¾ yards

• **Blue:** 1¾ yards

Solid gray cotton: ½ yard

Woven interfacing: 2 yards

Polyester quilt batting:
High loft, twin size

Zippers (2):

• 1 separating, 84″ long

• 1 with large teeth, 9″ long

Thread to match

Adhesive basting spray

Quilting pins

cutting

• Download and print the Sleep Sack patterns. (For downloading instructions, see Some Essentials for This Book, page 8.)

• Make templates from the patterns. Transfer all markings to the templates.

GRAY MINKY CUDDLE

• Cut 1 of Body.

• Cut 1 of Face.

WHITE MINKY CUDDLE

• Cut 2 of Eye.

NAVY MINKY CUDDLE

• Cut 2 of Eye Pupil.

SHARK-PRINT MINKY CUDDLE

• Cut 1 square 60″ × 60″ for exterior.

BLUE MINKY CUDDLE

• Cut 1 square 60″ × 60″ for lining.

GRAY COTTON

• Cut 2 rectangles 6″ × 10″ for pocket.

WOVEN INTERFACING

• Cut 1 of Body.

QUILT BATTING

• Cut 1 square 60″ × 60″.

make the shark appliqué

1. Apply adhesive basting spray to the Face.

2. Lay the Face over the woven interfacing, and smooth it so it sticks. Cut the interfacing around the Face.

3. Repeat this process for the Body.

4. Lay the Face over the Body where marked. Hand baste or pin securely.

5. With a close zigzag stitch, appliqué the Face to the Body.

6. From the wrong side, cut out the Body from within the stitches of the Face to eliminate bulk.

7. Apply adhesive spray to the Eyes and to the Eye Pupils. Lay them onto the woven interfacing and smooth them so they stick. Cut the interfacing around the Eyes and the Eye Pupils.

8. Lay the Pupils on the Eyes where marked on the pattern pieces. With a close zigzag stitch, appliqué the Pupils to the Eyes.

9. Lay the Eyes onto the Face where marked and, using a close zigzag stitch, appliqué the Eyes to the Face.

10. Lay the entire shark Body onto the right half of the shark-print minky cuddle. Arrange it so that it is pleasing to you, making certain that the edge of the shark is at least 2″ away from the right-hand edge of the shark-print minky cuddle. Refer to the project photo (previous page) for placement.

11. Hand baste or securely pin the Body onto the shark-print minky cuddle.

12. Using a close zigzag stitch, appliqué the Body to the shark-print minky cuddle.

13. Cut the shark-print minky cuddle out from behind the Face to eliminate bulk.

make the pocket

All seam allowances are ⅜″ unless otherwise noted.

NOTE: Refer to Zipper Anatomy (page 9) and mark "R" and "L" on the right and left halves of each of the two zipper tapes.

1. Lay a pocket rectangle over the right side of the Face where marked on the pattern.

2. Stitch on the markings for the pocket. Cut a slit inside the markings, being sure to clip to the corners.

3. Pull the pocket rectangle through the slit to the wrong side. With a pressing cloth and low iron heat, press the slit from the back so that the cotton from the pocket rectangle does not show from the front. Hand baste around the opening.

4. Lay the 9″ zipper tab side up under the opening. Baste or pin securely. From the front, stitch around the opening, making sure to catch the zipper sides in the stitching. Trim any excess zipper from beyond the stitching.

5. Turn the piece over and lay the second pocket rectangle over the sewn-in pocket rectangle, matching the edges. Stitch around all sides, keeping it free from the minky cuddle fabric.

make the sleep sack front

1. Layer the shark-print minky cuddle right side up onto the batting, matching the edges and smoothing continuously. Make certain that the pocket lies flat and in place.

2. Using long quilting pins, pin together the 2 layers, starting in the center and working outward. Pin approximately every 3″.

3. Quilt the 2 layers together from the center outward, using a wavy quilting pattern in rows from side to side. Stitch the rows about 6″ apart. Make sure *not* to stitch over the shark or pocket.

4. When you finish quilting, remove the pins and trim the batting even with the minky cuddle fabric.

sew the 84″ zipper

1. Mark the center edges on the sleep sack.

2. At the center of the sack, lay and pin the bottom of half of the separating zipper, with the zipper teeth facing inward toward the shark-print minky cuddle. Continue to pin it across the bottom, up the side, and across the top, rounding the corners. Hand baste in place.

3. Repeat Step 2 for the other half of the separating zipper, but pin and baste in the opposite direction on the sack.

4. Lay the minky cuddle lining right sides together with the shark-print minky cuddle. Hand baste or pin very securely around the entire perimeter of the sleep sack, making sure to catch the zipper tape.

5. Stitch around the entire perimeter, catching the zipper tape. Leave a 5″ opening at the top for turning right sides out. Trim the seam allowances on the inside of the sleep sack.

tip *In this case, it is helpful to use a walking foot rather than a zipper foot.*

6. Turn right sides out. Stitch the opening closed by hand or by machine.

7. Zip the sleep sack closed.

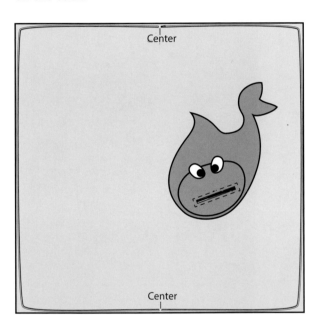

Fill the shark's mouth with a toothbrush and pajamas, and head over to Grandma's!

colorful floor pillow

• **Finished size:** 45″ wide × 52″ long × 11″ deep •

Throw yourself down on top of this wonderful pillow and watch your favorite show! This extra-large pillow would make a great spot for a baby during supervised playtime, or for a tuckered-out older child during naptime.

materials

Minky cuddle:

- **6 assorted colors:** ⅝ yard of *each* color

- **1 additional color:** 1½ yards for backing

Wide-back cotton or flannel: 108″ wide, 1½ yards

Sticky stabilizer: Such as Wash-Away Stitch Stabilizer (by C&T Publishing) or Sulky Sticky Fabri-Solvy Stabilizer

Polyester stuffing: 5 bags (24 ounces each)

Zipper: Nylon, 45″ long

Thread to match

cutting

- Download and print the Colorful Floor Pillow patterns. (For downloading instructions, see Some Essentials for This Book, page 8.)

- Make templates from the patterns. Transfer all markings to the templates.

ASSORTED COLORS MINKY CUDDLE

- Cut 6 of Piece B (3 and 3 reversed).

ADDITIONAL COLOR MINKY CUDDLE

- Cut 1 of Piece A.

COTTON OR FLANNEL

- Cut 2 of Piece A for pillow interior.

assemble the front

All seam allowances are ⅜″ unless otherwise noted.

1. Cut ½″ strips of sticky stabilizer and stick them to the edges that will be sewn. You can also stay stitch the edge or use your preferred stabilization method. Refer to How to Keep Fabric from Stretching (page 5).

2. Transfer all markings from the templates onto the fabric.

3. With right sides together, join 1 Piece B and 1 Piece B-reversed and pin securely. Stitch them together, stopping at the mark.

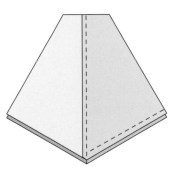

4. Repeat Step 3 twice more with the other Pieces B and B-reversed.

5. Join all pieces along the short angled edges, stopping at the marks. The last seam will be a slight set-in seam.

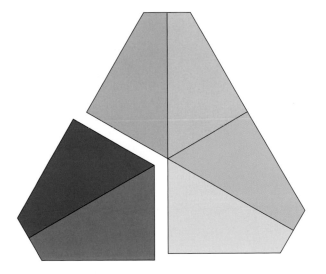

sew the zipper

NOTE: Refer to Zipper Anatomy (page 9) and mark "R" and "L" on the right and left halves of the zipper tape.

1. Lay the left half of the zipper facedown along an edge of the pillow front, keeping the edges together. Stitch the zipper tape.

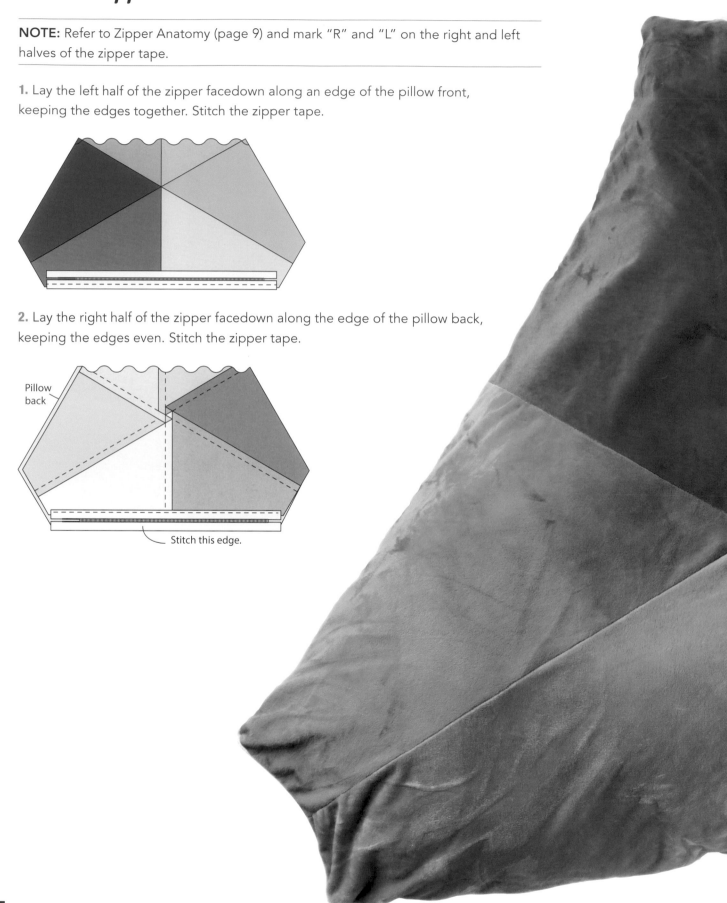

2. Lay the right half of the zipper facedown along the edge of the pillow back, keeping the edges even. Stitch the zipper tape.

Pillow back

Stitch this edge.

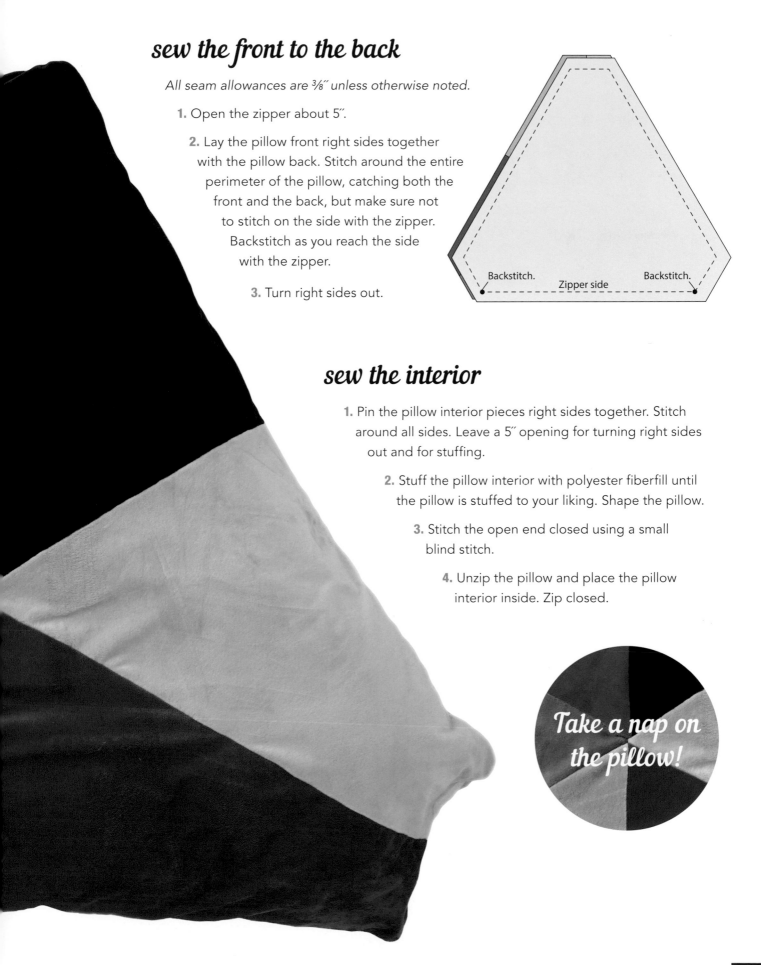

sew the front to the back

All seam allowances are ⅜″ unless otherwise noted.

1. Open the zipper about 5″.

2. Lay the pillow front right sides together with the pillow back. Stitch around the entire perimeter of the pillow, catching both the front and the back, but make sure not to stitch on the side with the zipper. Backstitch as you reach the side with the zipper.

3. Turn right sides out.

Backstitch.   Zipper side   Backstitch.

sew the interior

1. Pin the pillow interior pieces right sides together. Stitch around all sides. Leave a 5″ opening for turning right sides out and for stuffing.

2. Stuff the pillow interior with polyester fiberfill until the pillow is stuffed to your liking. Shape the pillow.

3. Stitch the open end closed using a small blind stitch.

4. Unzip the pillow and place the pillow interior inside. Zip closed.

Take a nap on the pillow!

cuddle me cuttlefish

• **Finished size:** 45″ × 56″ •

Cuttlefish are ocean animals of the order Sepiida. The overarching class is Cephalopoda, which includes squids and octopuses! What a great name for a quilt that will cuddle you to sleep!

materials

Minky cuddle:

- **Navy:** ½ yard

- **Blush-colored dimple:** ½ yard

- **White:** ½ yard

- **Green:** ½ yard

- **Turquoise:** 1½ yard

Fusible woven interfacing: 2 yards

Quilt backing: 4 yards

Quilt batting: Twin size

cutting

- Download and print the *Cuddle Me Cuttlefish* patterns. (For downloading instructions, see Some Essentials for This Book, page 8.)

- Make templates from the patterns. Transfer all markings to the templates.

NAVY MINKY CUDDLE

- Cut 1 of Large Wave.

- Cut 2 of Octopus Eye Pupil.

BLUSH DIMPLE MINKY CUDDLE

- Cut 1 of Octopus Head.

- Cut 3 of Octopus Leg A (2 and 1 reversed).

- Cut 1 of Octopus Leg B.

- Cut 1 of Octopus Leg C.

WHITE MINKY CUDDLE

- Cut 1 rectangle 18˝ × 45˝.

- Cut 2 of Octopus Eye.

GREEN MINKY CUDDLE

- Cut 1 of Small Wave.

TURQUOISE MINKY CUDDLE

- Cut 1 rectangle 39˝ × 45˝.

make the background

All seam allowances are ⅜˝ unless otherwise noted.

With right sides together, stitch the white minky cuddle rectangle to the turquoise minky cuddle rectangle along the 45˝ edge. The background should measure 45˝ × 56˝.

make the waves

1. Lay the Large Wave with the wrong side against the fusible side of the fusible woven interfacing. Turn over so that the interfacing is on top. Using an iron on low heat setting, fuse the interfacing to the wave.

2. Cut the interfacing away at the edges of the wave.

3. Using the quilt photo (previous page, bottom left) as a guide, lay the wave over the background, making sure that the high points of the wave overlap the seamline of the background pieces.

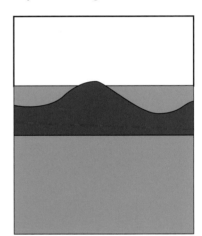

4. Hand baste or securely pin the wave in place.

5. Using a zigzag stitch, appliqué the wave to the background.

6. Repeat the fusing interfacing method in Steps 1 and 2 for the Small Wave, Octopus Eyes, Octopus Eye Pupils, Octopus Head, and Octopus Legs.

7. Using a zigzag stitch, appliqué the Octopus Eye Pupils to the Octopus Eyes where marked on the pattern.

8. Using a zigzag stitch, appliqué the Octopus Eyes to the Octopus Head.

9. Referring to the quilt photo, place the Octopus Legs and Octopus Head. Hand baste in place securely.

tip *In this case, hand basting works better than pinning, as this quilt is built in layers. The pieces can be pinned, but it makes it much more difficult.*

10. Lay the Small Wave over the octopus pieces and hand baste in place. Using a zigzag stitch, appliqué all pieces to the quilt, starting with the octopus pieces and finishing with the Small Wave.

finish the quilt

1. Layer the quilt top with batting and backing.

2. Quilt and bind, referring to Nontraditional Binding (page 11) or using your preferred method.

about the author

ALSO BY JUDY GAUTHIER

Judy Gauthier is the owner of Bungalow Quilting & Yarn in Ripon, Wisconsin. She is the author of two books, *Quilts for Scrap Lovers* and *Rainbow Quilts for Scrap Lovers*, both from C&T Publishing. She has been sewing most of her life. Judy always says for her, it's all about the color and the fabric, but design has become a favorite pastime. She is also a critical care registered nurse, mother to four grown children, and wife of 30 years. She resides in Ripon, Wisconsin.

Visit Judy online!

Website: bungalowquilting.com   •   **Instagram:** @bungalowquilting

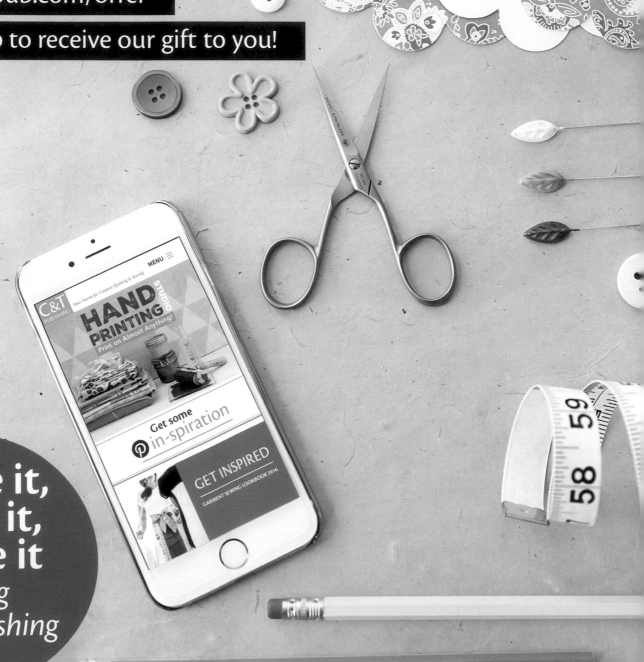

Want even more creative content?

Make it,
snap it,
share it
using
#ctpublishing